General William Booth enters into Heaven and other Poems

Vachel Lindsay

Contents

General William Booth Enters into Heaven 7
The Drunkards in the Street 10
The City That Will Not Repent 10
The Trap 13
Where is David, the Next King of Israel? 15
On Reading Omar Khayyam 16
The Beggar's Valentine 18
Honor Among Scamps 20
The Gamblers 21
On the Road to Nowhere 22
Upon Returning to the Country Road 24
The Angel and the Clown 25
Springfield Magical 26
Incense 26
The Wedding of the Rose and the Lotos 27
King Arthur's Men Have Come Again 28
Foreign Missions in Battle Array 29
Star of My Heart 30
Look You, I'll Go Pray 31
At Mass 32
Heart of God 32
The Empty Boats 33
With a Bouquet of Twelve Roses 33
St. Francis of Assisi 34
Buddha 34
A Prayer to All the Dead Among Mine Own People 35
To Reformers in Despair 35
Why I Voted the Socialist Ticket 35
To the United States Senate 37
The Knight in Disguise 39
The Wizard in the Street 41
The Eagle that is Forgotten 43
Shakespeare 44
Michelangelo 44
Titian 45
Lincoln 45
The Cornfields 46
Sweet Briars of the Stairways 46
Fantasies and Whims:-- 48
The Fairy Bridal Hymn 48
The Potato's Dance 49
How a Little Girl Sang 50
Ghosts in Love 51
The Queen of Bubbles 51
The Tree of Laughing Bells, or The Wings of the Morning 52
The Indian Girl Who Made Them 53
The Indian Girl Tells the Hero Where to Go to Get the Laughing Bell 53
The Journey Starts Swiftly 55
He Nears the Goal 55
He Climbs the Hill Where the Tree Grows 56
He Starts on the Return Journey 57

He Gives What He Won to the Indian Girl 58
 Sweetheart Spring 59
Sweetheart Summer 59
Sweetheart Autumn 60
Sweetheart Winter 60
The Sorceress! 61
Caught in a Net 61
Eden in Winter 62
Genesis 65
Queen Mab in the Village 67
The Dandelion 70
The Light o' the Moon 71
The Old Horse in the City 71
What the Hyena Said 72
What the Snow Man Said 72
What the Scare-crow Said 73
What Grandpa Mouse Said 74
The Beggar Speaks 74
What the Forester Said 75
A Net to Snare the Moonlight 76
Beyond the Moon 77
The Song of the Garden-Toad 78
A Gospel of Beauty:-- 79
The Proud Farmer 79
The Illinois Village 81
On the Building of Springfield 83

GENERAL WILLIAM BOOTH
ENTERS INTO HEAVEN
AND OTHER POEMS

BY

Vachel Lindsay

General William Booth Enters into Heaven

[To be sung to the tune of 'The Blood of the Lamb' with indicated instrument]

I

[Bass drum beaten loudly.]
Booth led boldly with his big bass drum--
(Are you washed in the blood of the Lamb?)
The Saints smiled gravely and they said: "He's come."
(Are you washed in the blood of the Lamb?)
Walking lepers followed, rank on rank,
Lurching bravoes from the ditches dank,
Drabs from the alleyways and drug fiends pale--
Minds still passion-ridden, soul-powers frail:--
Vermin-eaten saints with mouldy breath,
Unwashed legions with the ways of Death--
(Are you washed in the blood of the Lamb?)

[Banjos.]
Every slum had sent its half-a-score
The round world over. (Booth had groaned for more.)
Every banner that the wide world flies
Bloomed with glory and transcendent dyes.
Big-voiced lasses made their banjos bang,

Tranced, fanatical they shrieked and sang:--
"Are you washed in the blood of the Lamb?"
Hallelujah! It was queer to see
Bull-necked convicts with that land make free.
Loons with trumpets blowed a blare, blare, blare
On, on upward thro' the golden air!
(Are you washed in the blood of the Lamb?)

   II

 [Bass drum slower and softer.]
Booth died blind and still by Faith he trod,
Eyes still dazzled by the ways of God.
Booth led boldly, and he looked the chief
Eagle countenance in sharp relief,
Beard a-flying, air of high command
Unabated in that holy land.

 [Sweet flute music.]
Jesus came from out the court-house door,
Stretched his hands above the passing poor.
Booth saw not, but led his queer ones there
Round and round the mighty court-house square.
Yet in an instant all that blear review
Marched on spotless, clad in raiment new.
The lame were straightened, withered limbs uncurled
And blind eyes opened on a new, sweet world.

 [Bass drum louder.]
Drabs and vixens in a flash made whole!
Gone was the weasel-head, the snout, the jowl!
Sages and sibyls now, and athletes clean,

Rulers of empires, and of forests green!

[Grand chorus of all instruments. Tambourines to the foreground.]
The hosts were sandalled, and their wings were fire!
(Are you washed in the blood of the Lamb?)
But their noise played havoc with the angel-choir.
(Are you washed in the blood of the Lamb?)
O, shout Salvation! It was good to see
Kings and Princes by the Lamb set free.
The banjos rattled and the tambourines
Jing-jing-jingled in the hands of Queens.

[Reverently sung, no instruments.]
And when Booth halted by the curb for prayer
He saw his Master thro' the flag-filled air.
Christ came gently with a robe and crown
For Booth the soldier, while the throng knelt down.
He saw King Jesus. They were face to face,
And he knelt a-weeping in that holy place.
Are you washed in the blood of the Lamb?

The Drunkards in the Street

The Drunkards in the street are calling one another,
Heeding not the night-wind, great of heart and gay,--
Publicans and wantons--
Calling, laughing, calling,
While the Spirit bloweth Space and Time away.

Why should I feel the sobbing, the secrecy, the glory,
This comforter, this fitful wind divine?
I the cautious Pharisee, the scribe, the whited sepulchre--
I have no right to God, he is not mine.

          *   *   *   *   *

Within their gutters, drunkards dream of Hell.
I say my prayers by my white bed to-night,
With the arms of God about me, with the angels singing, singing
Until the grayness of my soul grows white.

The City That Will Not Repent

Climbing the heights of Berkeley
Nightly I watch the West.
There lies new San Francisco,
Sea-maid in purple dressed,
Wearing a dancer's girdle
All to inflame desire:

Scorning her days of sackcloth,
Scorning her cleansing fire.

See, like a burning city
Sets now the red sun's dome.
See, mystic firebrands sparkle
There on each store and home.
See how the golden gateway
Burns with the day to be--
Torch-bearing fiends of portent
Loom o'er the earth and sea.

Not by the earthquake daunted
Nor by new fears made tame,
Painting her face and laughing
Plays she a new-found game.
Here on her half-cool cinders
'Frisco abides in mirth,
Planning the wildest splendor
Ever upon the earth.

Here on this crumbling rock-ledge
'Frisco her all will stake,
Blowing her bubble-towers,
Swearing they will not break,
Rearing her Fair transcendent,
Singing with piercing art,
Calling to Ancient Asia,
Wooing young Europe's heart.
Here where her God has scourged her
Wantoning, singing sweet:
Waiting her mad bad lovers
Here by the judgment-seat!

'Frisco, God's doughty foeman,
Scorns and blasphemes him strong.
Tho' he again should smite her
She would not slack her song.
Nay, she would shriek and rally--
'Frisco would ten times rise!
Not till her last tower crumbles,
Not till her last rose dies,
Not till the coast sinks seaward,
Not till the cold tides beat
Over the high white Shasta,
'Frisco will cry defeat.

God loves this rebel city,
Loves foemen brisk and game,
Tho', just to please the angels,
He may send down his flame.
God loves the golden leopard
Tho' he may spoil her lair.
God smites, yet loves the lion.
God makes the panther fair.

Dance then, wild guests of 'Frisco,
Yellow, bronze, white and red!
Dance by the golden gateway--
Dance, tho' he smite you dead!

The Trap

She was taught desire in the street,
Not at the angels' feet.
By the good no word was said
Of the worth of the bridal bed.
The secret was learned from the vile,
Not from her mother's smile.
Home spoke not. And the girl
Was caught in the public whirl.
Do you say "She gave consent:
Life drunk, she was content
With beasts that her fire could please?"
But she did not choose disease
Of mind and nerves and breath.
She was trapped to a slow, foul death.
The door was watched so well,
That the steep dark stair to hell
Was the only escaping way . . .
"She gave consent," you say?

Some think she was meek and good,
Only lost in the wood
Of youth, and deceived in man
When the hunger of sex began
That ties the husband and wife
To the end in a strong fond life.
Her captor, by chance was one
Of those whose passion was done,
A cold fierce worm of the sea
Enslaving for you and me.

The wages the poor must take
Have forced them to serve this snake.
Yea, half-paid girls must go
For bread to his pit below.
What hangman shall wait his host
Of butchers from coast to coast,
New York to the Golden Gate--
The merger of death and fate,
Lust-kings with a careful plan
Clean-cut, American?

In liberty's name we cry
For these women about to die.

O mothers who failed to tell
The mazes of heaven and hell,
Who failed to advise, implore
Your daughters at Love's strange door,
What will you do this day?
Your dear ones are hidden away,
As good as chained to the bed,
Hid like the mad, or the dead:--
The glories of endless years
Drowned in their harlot-tears:
The children they hoped to bear,
Grandchildren strong and fair,
The life for ages to be,
Cut off like a blasted tree,
Murdered in filth in a day,
Somehow, by the merchant gay!

In liberty's name we cry
For these women about to die.

What shall be said of a state
Where traps for the white brides wait?
Of sellers of drink who play
The game for the extra pay?
Of statesmen in league with all
Who hope for the girl-child's fall?
Of banks where hell's money is paid
And Pharisees all afraid
Of pandars that help them sin?
When will our wrath begin?

Where is David, the Next King of Israel?

Where is David? . . . O God's people,
Saul has passed, the good and great.
Mourn for Saul the first-anointed--
Head and shoulders o'er the state.

He was found among the Prophets:
Judge and monarch, merged in one.
But the wars of Saul are ended
And the works of Saul are done.

Where is David, ruddy shepherd,
God's boy-king for Israel?
Mystic, ardent, dowered with beauty,
Singing where still waters dwell?

Prophet, find that destined minstrel
Wandering on the range to-day,
Driving sheep and crooning softly

Psalms that cannot pass away.

"David waits," the prophet answers,
"In a black notorious den,
In a cave upon the border
With four hundred outlaw men.

"He is fair, and loved of women,
Mighty-hearted, born to sing:
Thieving, weeping, erring, praying,
Radiant royal rebel-king.

"He will come with harp and psaltry,
Quell his troop of convict swine,
Quell his mad-dog roaring rascals,
Witching them with words divine--

   "They will ram the walls of Zion!
   They will win us Salem hill,
   All for David, Shepherd David--
   Singing like a mountain rill!"

On Reading Omar Khayyam

[During an anti-saloon campaign, in central Illinois.]

In the midst of the battle I turned,
(For the thunders could flourish without me)
And hid by a rose-hung wall,
Forgetting the murder about me;
And wrote, from my wound, on the stone,

In mirth, half prayer, half play:--
"Send me a picture book,
Send me a song, to-day."

I saw him there by the wall
When I scarce had written the line,
In the enemy's colors dressed
And the serpent-standard of wine
Writhing its withered length
From his ghostly hands o'er the ground,
And there by his shadowy breast
The glorious poem I found.

This was his world-old cry:
Thus read the famous prayer:
"Wine, wine, wine and flowers
And cup-bearers always fair!"
'Twas a book of the snares of earth
Bordered in gold and blue,
And I read each line to the wind
And read to the roses too:
And they nodded their womanly heads
And told to the wall just why
For wine of the earth men bleed,
Kingdoms and empires die.
I envied the grape stained sage:
(The roses were praising him.)
The ways of the world seemed good
And the glory of heaven dim.
I envied the endless kings
Who found great pearls in the mire,
Who bought with the nation's life
The cup of delicious fire.

But the wine of God came down,
And I drank it out of the air.
(Fair is the serpent-cup,
But the cup of God more fair.)
The wine of God came down
That makes no drinker to weep.
And I went back to battle again
Leaving the singer asleep.

The Beggar's Valentine

Kiss me and comfort my heart
  Maiden honest and fine.
I am the pilgrim boy
  Lame, but hunting the shrine;

Fleeing away from the sweets,
  Seeking the dust and rain,
Sworn to the staff and road,
  Scorning pleasure and pain;

Nevertheless my mouth
  Would rest like a bird an hour
And find in your curls a nest
  And find in your breast a bower:

Nevertheless my eyes
  Would lose themselves in your own,
Rivers that seek the sea,
  Angels before the throne:

Kiss me and comfort my heart,
 For love can never be mine:
Passion, hunger and pain,
 These are the only wine

Of the pilgrim bound to the road.
 He would rob no man of his own.
Your heart is another's I know,
 Your honor is his alone.

The feasts of a long drawn love,
 The feasts of a wedded life,
The harvests of patient years,
 And hearthstone and children and wife:

These are your lords I know.
 These can never be mine--
This is the price I pay
 For the foolish search for the shrine:

This is the price I pay
 For the joy of my midnight prayers,
Kneeling beneath the moon
 With hills for my altar stairs;

This is the price I pay
 For the throb of the mystic wings,
When the dove of God comes down
 And beats round my heart and sings;

This is the price I pay
 For the light I shall some day see
At the ends of the infinite earth

When truth shall come to me.

And what if my body die
 Before I meet the truth?
The road is dear, more dear
 Than love or life or youth.

The road, it is the road,
 Mystical, endless, kind,
Mother of visions vast,
 Mother of soul and mind;

Mother of all of me
 But the blood that cries for a mate--
That cries for a farewell kiss
 From the child of God at the gate.

Honor Among Scamps

We are the smirched. Queen Honor is the spotless.
We slept thro' wars where Honor could not sleep.
We were faint-hearted. Honor was full-valiant.
We kept a silence Honor could not keep.

Yet this late day we make a song to praise her.
We, codeless, will yet vindicate her code.
She who was mighty, walks with us, the beggars.
The merchants drive her out upon the road.

She makes a throne of sod beside our campfire.
We give the maiden-queen our rags and tears.

A battered, rascal guard have rallied round her,
To keep her safe until the better years.

The Gamblers

Life's a jail where men have common lot.
Gaunt the one who has, and who has not.
All our treasures neither less nor more,
Bread alone comes thro' the guarded door.
Cards are foolish in this jail, I think,
Yet they play for shoes, for drabs and drink.
She, my lawless, sharp-tongued gypsy maid
Will not scorn with me this jail-bird trade,
Pets some fox-eyed boy who turns the trick,
Tho' he win a button or a stick,
Pencil, garter, ribbon, corset-lace--
HIS the glory, MINE is the disgrace.

Sweet, I'd rather lose than win despite
Love of hearty words and maids polite.
"Love's a gamble," say you. I deny.
Love's a gift. I love you till I die.
Gamblers fight like rats. I will not play.
All I ever had I gave away.
All I ever coveted was peace
Such as comes if we have jail release.
Cards are puzzles, tho' the prize be gold,
Cards help not the bread that tastes of mold,
Cards dye not your hair to black more deep,
Cards make not the children cease to weep.

Scorned, I sit with half shut eyes all day--
Watch the cataract of sunshine play
Down the wall, and dance upon the floor.
Sun, come down and break the dungeon door!
Of such gold dust could I make a key,--
Turn the bolt--how soon we would be free!
Over borders we would hurry on
Safe by sunrise farms, and springs of dawn,
Wash our wounds and jail stains there at last,
Azure rivers flowing, flowing past.
GOD HAS GREAT ESTATES JUST PAST THE LINE,
GREEN FARMS FOR ALL, AND MEAT AND CORN AND WINE.

On the Road to Nowhere

On the road to nowhere
What wild oats did you sow
When you left your father's house
With your cheeks aglow?
Eyes so strained and eager
To see what you might see?
Were you thief or were you fool
Or most nobly free?

Were the tramp-days knightly,
True sowing of wild seed?
Did you dare to make the songs
Vanquished workmen need?
Did you waste much money
To deck a leper's feast?
Love the truth, defy the crowd

Scandalize the priest?
On the road to nowhere
What wild oats did you sow?
Stupids find the nowhere-road
Dusty, grim and slow.

Ere their sowing's ended
They turn them on their track,
Look at the caitiff craven wights
Repentant, hurrying back!
Grown ashamed of nowhere,
Of rags endured for years,
Lust for velvet in their hearts,
Pierced with Mammon's spears,
All but a few fanatics
Give up their darling goal,
Seek to be as others are,
Stultify the soul.
Reapings now confront them,
Glut them, or destroy,
Curious seeds, grain or weeds
Sown with awful joy.
Hurried is their harvest,
They make soft peace with men.
Pilgrims pass. They care not,
Will not tramp again.

O nowhere, golden nowhere!
Sages and fools go on
To your chaotic ocean,
To your tremendous dawn.
Far in your fair dream-haven,
Is nothing or is all . . .

They press on, singing, sowing
Wild deeds without recall!

Upon Returning to the Country Road

Even the shrewd and bitter,
Gnarled by the old world's greed,
Cherished the stranger softly
Seeing his utter need.
Shelter and patient hearing,
These were their gifts to him,
To the minstrel, grimly begging
As the sunset-fire grew dim.
The rich said "You are welcome."
Yea, even the rich were good.
How strange that in their feasting
His songs were understood!
The doors of the poor were open,
The poor who had wandered too,
Who had slept with ne'er a roof-tree
Under the wind and dew.
The minds of the poor were open,
Their dark mistrust was dead.
They loved his wizard stories,
They bought his rhymes with bread.
Those were his days of glory,
Of faith in his fellow-men.
Therefore, to-day the singer
Turns beggar once again.

The Angel and the Clown

I saw wild domes and bowers
And smoking incense towers
And mad exotic flowers
In Illinois.
Where ragged ditches ran
Now springs of Heaven began
Celestial drink for man
In Illinois.

There stood beside the town
Beneath its incense-crown
An angel and a clown
In Illinois.
He was as Clowns are:
She was snow and star
With eyes that looked afar
In Illinois.

I asked, "How came this place
Of antique Asian grace
Amid our callow race
In Illinois?"
Said Clown and Angel fair:
"By laughter and by prayer,
By casting off all care
In Illinois."

Springfield Magical

In this, the City of my Discontent,
Sometimes there comes a whisper from the grass,
"Romance, Romance--is here. No Hindu town
Is quite so strange. No Citadel of Brass
By Sinbad found, held half such love and hate;
No picture-palace in a picture-book
Such webs of Friendship, Beauty, Greed and Fate!"

In this, the City of my Discontent,
Down from the sky, up from the smoking deep
Wild legends new and old burn round my bed
While trees and grass and men are wrapped in sleep.
Angels come down, with Christmas in their hearts,
Gentle, whimsical, laughing, heaven-sent;
And, for a day, fair Peace have given me
In this, the City of my Discontent!

Incense

Think not that incense-smoke has had its day.
My friends, the incense-time has but begun.
Creed upon creed, cult upon cult shall bloom,
Shrine after shrine grow gray beneath the sun.

And mountain-boulders in our aged West
Shall guard the graves of hermits truth-endowed:

And there the scholar from the Chinese hills
Shall do deep honor, with his wise head bowed.

And on our old, old plains some muddy stream,
Dark as the Ganges, shall, like that strange tide--
(Whispering mystery to half the earth)--
Gather the praying millions to its side,

And flow past halls with statues in white stone
To saints unborn to-day, whose lives of grace
Shall make one shining, universal church
Where all Faiths kneel, as brothers, in one place.

The Wedding of the Rose and the Lotos

The wide Pacific waters
 And the Atlantic meet.
With cries of joy they mingle,
In tides of love they greet.
Above the drowned ages
A wind of wooing blows:--
The red rose woos the lotos,
The lotos woos the rose . . .

The lotos conquered Egypt.
 The rose was loved in Rome.
Great India crowned the lotos:
(Britain the rose's home).
Old China crowned the lotos,
They crowned it in Japan.
But Christendom adored the rose

Ere Christendom began . . .

The lotos speaks of slumber:
The rose is as a dart.
 The lotos is Nirvana:
The rose is Mary's heart.
The rose is deathless, restless,
The splendor of our pain:
 The flush and fire of labor
That builds, not all in vain. . . .

The genius of the lotos
Shall heal earth's too-much fret.
The rose, in blinding glory,
Shall waken Asia yet.
Hail to their loves, ye peoples!
Behold, a world-wind blows,
That aids the ivory lotos
To wed the red red rose!

King Arthur's Men Have Come Again

[Written while a field-worker in the Anti-Saloon League of Illinois.]

King Arthur's men have come again.
They challenge everywhere
The foes of Christ's Eternal Church.
Her incense crowns the air.
The heathen knighthood cower and curse
To hear the bugles ring,
BUT SPEARS ARE SET, THE CHARGE IS ON,

WISE ARTHUR SHALL BE KING!

And Cromwell's men have come again,
I meet them in the street.
Stern but in this--no way of thorns
Shall snare the children's feet.
The reveling foemen wreak but waste,
A sodden poisonous band.
FIERCE CROMWELL BUILDS THE FLOWER-BRIGHT TOWNS,
AND A MORE SUNLIT LAND!

And Lincoln's men have come again.
Up from the South he flayed,
The grandsons of his foes arise
In his own cause arrayed.
They rise for freedom and clean laws
High laws, that shall endure.
OUR GOD ESTABLISHES HIS ARM
AND MAKES THE BATTLE SURE!

Foreign Missions in Battle Array

An endless line of splendor,
These troops with heaven for home,
With creeds they go from Scotland,
With incense go from Rome.
These, in the name of Jesus,
Against the dark gods stand,
They gird the earth with valor,
They heed their King's command.

Onward the line advances,
Shaking the hills with power,
Slaying the hidden demons,
The lions that devour.
No bloodshed in the wrestling,--
But souls new-born arise--
The nations growing kinder,
The child-hearts growing wise.

What is the final ending?
The issue, can we know?
Will Christ outlive Mohammed?
Will Kali's altar go?
This is our faith tremendous,--
Our wild hope, who shall scorn,--
That in the name of Jesus
The world shall be reborn!

Star of My Heart

Star of my heart, I follow from afar.
Sweet Love on high, lead on where shepherds are,
Where Time is not, and only dreamers are.
Star from of old, the Magi-Kings are dead
And a foolish Saxon seeks the manger-bed.
O lead me to Jehovah's child
Across this dreamland lone and wild,
Then will I speak this prayer unsaid,
And kiss his little haloed head--
"My star and I, we love thee, little child."

Except the Christ be born again to-night
In dreams of all men, saints and sons of shame,
The world will never see his kingdom bright.
Stars of all hearts, lead onward thro' the night
Past death-black deserts, doubts without a name,
Past hills of pain and mountains of new sin
To that far sky where mystic births begin,
Where dreaming ears the angel-song shall win.
Our Christmas shall be rare at dawning there,
And each shall find his brother fair,
Like a little child within:
All hearts of the earth shall find new birth
And wake, no more to sin.

Look You, I'll Go Pray

Look you, I'll go pray,
My shame is crying,
My soul is gray and faint,
My faith is dying.
Look you, I'll go pray--
"Sweet Mary, make me clean,
Thou rainstorm of the soul,
Thou wine from worlds unseen."

At Mass

No doubt to-morrow I will hide
My face from you, my King.
Let me rejoice this Sunday noon,
And kneel while gray priests sing.

It is not wisdom to forget.
But since it is my fate
Fill thou my soul with hidden wine
To make this white hour great.

My God, my God, this marvelous hour
I am your son I know.
Once in a thousand days your voice
Has laid temptation low.

Heart of God

O great heart of God,
Once vague and lost to me,
Why do I throb with your throb to-night,
In this land, eternity?

O little heart of God,
Sweet intruding stranger,
You are laughing in my human breast,
A Christ-child in a manger.

Heart, dear heart of God,
Beside you now I kneel,
Strong heart of faith. O heart not mine,
Where God has set His seal.

Wild thundering heart of God
Out of my doubt I come,
And my foolish feet with prophets' feet,
March with the prophets' drum.

The Empty Boats

Why do I see these empty boats, sailing on airy seas?
One haunted me the whole night long, swaying with every breeze,
Returning always near the eaves, or by the skylight glass:
There it will wait me many weeks, and then, at last, will pass.
Each soul is haunted by a ship in which that soul might ride
And climb the glorious mysteries of Heaven's silent tide
In voyages that change the very metes and bounds of Fate--
O empty boats, we all refuse, that by our windows wait!

With a Bouquet of Twelve Roses

I saw Lord Buddha towering by my gate
Saying: "Once more, good youth, I stand and wait."
Saying: "I bring you my fair Law of Peace
And from your withering passion full release;

Release from that white hand that stabbed you so.
The road is calling. With the wind you go,
Forgetting her imperious disdain--
Quenching all memory in the sun and rain."

"Excellent Lord, I come. But first," I said,
"Grant that I bring her these twelve roses red.
Yea, twelve flower kisses for her rose-leaf mouth,
And then indeed I go in bitter drouth
To that far valley where your river flows
In Peace, that once I found in every rose."

St. Francis of Assisi

Would I might wake St. Francis in you all,
Brother of birds and trees, God's Troubadour,
Blinded with weeping for the sad and poor;
Our wealth undone, all strict Franciscan men,
Come, let us chant the canticle again
Of mother earth and the enduring sun.
God make each soul the lonely leper's slave;
God make us saints, and brave.

Buddha

Would that by Hindu magic we became
Dark monks of jeweled India long ago,
Sitting at Prince Siddartha's feet to know

The foolishness of gold and love and station,
The gospel of the Great Renunciation,
The ragged cloak, the staff, the rain and sun,
The beggar's life, with far Nirvana gleaming:
Lord, make us Buddhas, dreaming.

A Prayer to All the Dead Among Mine Own People

Are these your presences, my clan from Heaven?
Are these your hands upon my wounded soul?
Mine own, mine own, blood of my blood be with me,
Fly by my path till you have made me whole!

To Reformers in Despair

'Tis not too late to build our young land right,
Cleaner than Holland, courtlier than Japan,
Devout like early Rome, with hearths like hers,
Hearths that will recreate the breed called man.

Why I Voted the Socialist Ticket

I am unjust, but I can strive for justice.
My life's unkind, but I can vote for kindness.
I, the unloving, say life should be lovely.
I, that am blind, cry out against my blindness.

Man is a curious brute--he pets his fancies--
Fighting mankind, to win sweet luxury.
So he will be, tho' law be clear as crystal,
Tho' all men plan to live in harmony.

Come, let us vote against our human nature,
Crying to God in all the polling places
To heal our everlasting sinfulness
And make us sages with transfigured faces.

The following verses were written on the evening of March the first,
nineteen hundred and eleven, and printed next morning
in the Illinois State Register.

They celebrate the arrival of the news that the United States Senate
had declared the election of William Lorimer good and valid,
by a vote of forty-six to forty.

To the United States Senate

[Revelation 16: Verses 16-19]

And must the Senator from Illinois
Be this squat thing, with blinking, half-closed eyes?
This brazen gutter idol, reared to power
Upon a leering pyramid of lies?

And must the Senator from Illinois
Be the world's proverb of successful shame,
Dazzling all State house flies that steal and steal,
Who, when the sad State spares them, count it fame?

If once or twice within his new won hall
His vote had counted for the broken men;
If in his early days he wrought some good--
We might a great soul's sins forgive him then.

But must the Senator from Illinois
Be vindicated by fat kings of gold?
And must he be belauded by the smirched,
The sleek, uncanny chiefs in lies grown old?

Be warned, O wanton ones, who shielded him--
Black wrath awaits. You all shall eat the dust.
You dare not say: "To-morrow will bring peace;
Let us make merry, and go forth in lust."

What will you trading frogs do on a day
When Armageddon thunders thro' the land;

When each sad patriot rises, mad with shame,
His ballot or his musket in his hand?

In the distracted states from which you came
The day is big with war hopes fierce and strange;
Our iron Chicagos and our grimy mines
Rumble with hate and love and solemn change.

Too many weary men shed honest tears,
Ground by machines that give the Senate ease.
Too many little babes with bleeding hands
Have heaped the fruits of empire on your knees.

And swine within the Senate in this day,
When all the smothering by-streets weep and wail;
When wisdom breaks the hearts of her best sons;
When kingly men, voting for truth, may fail:--

These are a portent and a call to arms.
Our protest turns into a battle cry:
"Our shame must end, our States be free and clean;
And in this war we choose to live and die."

[So far as the writer knows this is the first use
of the popular term Armageddon in present day politics.]

The Knight in Disguise

[Concerning O. Henry (Sidney Porter)]

"He could not forget that he was a Sidney."

Is this Sir Philip Sidney, this loud clown,
The darling of the glad and gaping town?

This is that dubious hero of the press
Whose slangy tongue and insolent address
Were spiced to rouse on Sunday afternoon
The man with yellow journals round him strewn.
We laughed and dozed, then roused and read again,
And vowed O. Henry funniest of men.
He always worked a triple-hinged surprise
To end the scene and make one rub his eyes.

He comes with vaudeville, with stare and leer.
He comes with megaphone and specious cheer.
His troupe, too fat or short or long or lean,
Step from the pages of the magazine
With slapstick or sombrero or with cane:
The rube, the cowboy or the masher vain.
They over-act each part. But at the height
Of banter and of canter and delight
The masks fall off for one queer instant there
And show real faces: faces full of care
And desperate longing: love that's hot or cold;
And subtle thoughts, and countenances bold.
The masks go back. 'Tis one more joke. Laugh on!

The goodly grown-up company is gone.

No doubt had he occasion to address
The brilliant court of purple-clad Queen Bess,
He would have wrought for them the best he knew
And led more loftily his actor-crew.
How coolly he misquoted. 'Twas his art--
Slave-scholar, who misquoted--from the heart.
So when we slapped his back with friendly roar
Aesop awaited him without the door,--
Aesop the Greek, who made dull masters laugh
With little tales of FOX and DOG and CALF.
And be it said, mid these his pranks so odd
With something nigh to chivalry he trod
And oft the drear and driven would defend--
The little shopgirls' knight unto the end.
Yea, he had passed, ere we could understand
The blade of Sidney glimmered in his hand.
Yea, ere we knew, Sir Philip's sword was drawn
With valiant cut and thrust, and he was gone.

The Wizard in the Street

[Concerning Edgar Allan Poe]

Who now will praise the Wizard in the street
With loyal songs, with humors grave and sweet--
This Jingle-man, of strolling players born,
Whom holy folk have hurried by in scorn,
This threadbare jester, neither wise nor good,
With melancholy bells upon his hood?

The hurrying great ones scorn his Raven's croak,
And well may mock his mystifying cloak
Inscribed with runes from tongues he has not read
To make the ignoramus turn his head.
The artificial glitter of his eyes
Has captured half-grown boys. They think him wise.
Some shallow player-folk esteem him deep,
Soothed by his steady wand's mesmeric sweep.
The little lacquered boxes in his hands
Somehow suggest old times and reverenced lands.
From them doll-monsters come, we know not how:
Puppets, with Cain's black rubric on the brow.
Some passing jugglers, smiling, now concede
That his best cabinet-work is made, indeed
By bleeding his right arm, day after day,
Triumphantly to seal and to inlay.
They praise his little act of shedding tears;
A trick, well learned, with patience, thro' the years.

I love him in this blatant, well-fed place.
Of all the faces, his the only face
Beautiful, tho' painted for the stage,
Lit up with song, then torn with cold, small rage,
Shames that are living, loves and hopes long dead,
Consuming pride, and hunger, real, for bread.

Here by the curb, ye Prophets thunder deep:
"What Nations sow, they must expect to reap,"
Or haste to clothe the race with truth and power,
With hymns and shouts increasing every hour.
Useful are you. There stands the useless one
Who builds the Haunted Palace in the sun.
Good tailors, can you dress a doll for me
With silks that whisper of the sounding sea?
One moment, citizens,--the weary tramp
Unveileth Psyche with the agate lamp.
Which one of you can spread a spotted cloak
And raise an unaccounted incense smoke
Until within the twilight of the day
Stands dark Ligeia in her disarray,
Witchcraft and desperate passion in her breath
And battling will, that conquers even death?

And now the evening goes. No man has thrown
The weary dog his well-earned crust or bone.
We grin and hie us home and go to sleep,
Or feast like kings till midnight, drinking deep.
He drank alone, for sorrow, and then slept,
And few there were that watched him, few that wept.
He found the gutter, lost to love and man.
Too slowly came the good Samaritan.

The Eagle that is Forgotten

[John P. Altgeld. Born Dec. 30, 1847; died March 12, 1902]

Sleep softly * * * eagle forgotten * * * under the stone.
Time has its way with you there, and the clay has its own.

"We have buried him now," thought your foes, and in secret rejoiced.
They made a brave show of their mourning, their hatred unvoiced.
They had snarled at you, barked at you, foamed at you day after day,
Now you were ended. They praised you, * * * and laid you away.

The others that mourned you in silence and terror and truth,
The widow bereft of her crust, and the boy without youth,
The mocked and the scorned and the wounded, the lame and the poor
That should have remembered forever, * * * remember no more.

Where are those lovers of yours, on what name do they call
The lost, that in armies wept over your funeral pall?
They call on the names of a hundred high-valiant ones,
A hundred white eagles have risen the sons of your sons,
The zeal in their wings is a zeal that your dreaming began
The valor that wore out your soul in the service of man.

Sleep softly, * * * eagle forgotten, * * * under the stone,
Time has its way with you there and the clay has its own.
Sleep on, O brave hearted, O wise man, that kindled the flame--
To live in mankind is far more than to live in a name,
To live in mankind, far, far more * * * than to live in a name.

Shakespeare

Would that in body and spirit Shakespeare came
Visible emperor of the deeds of Time,
With Justice still the genius of his rhyme,
Giving each man his due, each passion grace,
Impartial as the rain from Heaven's face
Or sunshine from the heaven-enthroned sun.
Sweet Swan of Avon, come to us again.
Teach us to write, and writing, to be men.

Michelangelo

Would I might wake in you the whirl-wind soul
Of Michelangelo, who hewed the stone
And Night and Day revealed, whose arm alone
Could draw the face of God, the titan high
Whose genius smote like lightning from the sky--
And shall he mold like dead leaves in the grave?
Nay he is in us! Let us dare and dare.
God help us to be brave.

Titian

Would that such hills and cities round us sang,
Such vistas of the actual earth and man
As kindled Titian when his life began;
Would that this latter Greek could put his gold,
Wisdom and splendor in our brushes bold
Till Greece and Venice, children of the sun,
Become our every-day, and we aspire
To colors fairer far, and glories higher.

Lincoln

Would I might rouse the Lincoln in you all,
That which is gendered in the wilderness
From lonely prairies and God's tenderness.
Imperial soul, star of a weedy stream,
Born where the ghosts of buffaloes still dream,
Whose spirit hoof-beats storm above his grave,
Above that breast of earth and prairie-fire--
Fire that freed the slave.

The Cornfields

The cornfields rise above mankind,
Lifting white torches to the blue,
Each season not ashamed to be
Magnificently decked for you.

What right have you to call them yours,
And in brute lust of riches burn
Without some radiant penance wrought,
Some beautiful, devout return?

Sweet Briars of the Stairways

We are happy all the time
Even when we fight:
Sweet briars of the stairways,
Gay fairies of the grime;
WE, WHO ARE PLAYING TO-NIGHT.

"Our feet are in the gutters,
Our eyes are sore with dust,
But still our eyes are bright.
The wide street roars and mutters--
We know it works because it must--
WE, WHO ARE PLAYING TO-NIGHT!

"Dirt is everlasting.-- We never, never fear it.

Toil is never ceasing.-- We will play until we near it.
Tears are never ending.-- When once real tears have come;

"When we see our people as they are--
Our fathers--broken, dumb--
Our mothers--broken, dumb--
The weariest of women and of men;
Ah--then our eyes will lose their light--
Then we will never play again--
　　WE, WHO ARE PLAYING TO-NIGHT."

Fantasies and Whims:--

The Fairy Bridal Hymn

[This is the hymn to Eleanor, daughter of Mab and a golden drone,
sung by the Locust choir when the fairy child marries her God,
the yellow rose]

This is a song to the white-armed one
Cold in the breast as the frost-wrapped Spring,
Whose feet are slow on the hills of life,
Whose round mouth rules by whispering.

This is a song to the white-armed one
Whose breast shall burn as a Summer field,
Whose wings shall rise to the doors of gold,
Whose poppy lips to the God shall yield.

This is a song to the white-armed one
When the closing rose shall bind her fast,
And a song of the song their blood shall sing,
When the Rose-God drinks her soul at last.

The Potato's Dance

"Down cellar," said the cricket,
"I saw a ball last night
In honor of a lady
Whose wings were pearly-white.
The breath of bitter weather
Had smashed the cellar pane:
We entertained a drift of leaves
And then of snow and rain.
But we were dressed for winter,
And loved to hear it blow
In honor of the lady
Who makes potatoes grow--
Our guest, the Irish lady,
The tiny Irish lady,
The fairy Irish lady
That makes potatoes grow.

"Potatoes were the waiters,
Potatoes were the band,
Potatoes were the dancers
Kicking up the sand:
Their legs were old burnt matches,
Their arms were just the same,
They jigged and whirled and scrambled
In honor of the dame:
The noble Irish lady
Who makes potatoes dance,
The witty Irish lady,
The saucy Irish lady,

The laughing Irish lady
Who makes potatoes prance.

"There was just one sweet potato.
He was golden-brown and slim:
The lady loved his figure.
She danced all night with him.
Alas, he wasn't Irish.
So when she flew away,
They threw him in the coal-bin
And there he is to-day,
Where they cannot hear his sighs--
His weeping for the lady,
The beauteous Irish lady,
The radiant Irish lady
Who gives potatoes eyes."

How a Little Girl Sang

Ah, she was music in herself,
A symphony of joyousness.
She sang, she sang from finger tips,
From every tremble of her dress.
I saw sweet haunting harmony,
An ecstasy, an ecstasy,
In that strange curling of her lips,
That happy curling of her lips.
And quivering with melody
Those eyes I saw, that tossing head.
And so I saw what music was,
Tho' still accursed with ears of lead.

Ghosts in Love

"Tell me, where do ghosts in love
Find their bridal veils?"

"If you and I were ghosts in love
We'd climb the cliffs of Mystery,
Above the sea of Wails.
I'd trim your gray and streaming hair
With veils of Fantasy
From the tree of Memory.
'Tis there the ghosts that fall in love
Find their bridal veils."

The Queen of Bubbles

[Written for a picture]

The Youth speaks:--
 "Why do you seek the sun
 In your bubble-crown ascending?
 Your chariot will melt to mist.
 Your crown will have an ending."

The Goddess replies:--
 "Nay, sun is but a bubble,
 Earth is a whiff of foam--
 To my caves on the coast of Thule

Each night I call them home.
Thence Faiths blow forth to angels
And loves blow forth to men--
They break and turn to nothing
And I make them whole again.
On the crested waves of chaos
I ride them back reborn:
New stars I bring at evening
For those that burst at morn:
My soul is the wind of Thule
And evening is the sign--
The sun is but a bubble,
A fragile child of mine."

The Tree of Laughing Bells, or The Wings of the Morning

[A Poem for Aviators]

How the Wings Were Made

From many morning-glories
That in an hour will fade,
From many pansy buds
Gathered in the shade,
From lily of the valley
And dandelion buds,
From fiery poppy-buds
 Are the Wings of the Morning made.

The Indian Girl Who Made Them

These, the Wings of the Morning,
An Indian Maiden wove,
Intertwining subtilely
Wands from a willow grove
Beside the Sangamon--
Rude stream of Dreamland Town.
She bound them to my shoulders
With fingers golden-brown.
The wings were part of me;
The willow-wands were hot.
Pulses from my heart
Healed each bruise and spot
Of the morning-glory buds,
Beginning to unfold
Beneath her burning song of suns untold.

The Indian Girl Tells the Hero Where to Go to Get the Laughing Bell

"To the farthest star of all,
Go, make a moment's raid.
To the west--escape the earth
Before your pennons fade!
West! west! o'ertake the night
That flees the morning sun.
There's a path between the stars--
A black and silent one.
O tremble when you near

The smallest star that sings:
Only the farthest star
Is cool for willow wings.

"There's a sky within the west--
There's a sky beyond the skies
Where only one star shines--
The Star of Laughing Bells--
In Chaos-land it lies;
Cold as morning-dew,
A gray and tiny boat
Moored on Chaos-shore,
Where nothing else can float
But the Wings of the Morning strong
And the lilt of laughing song
From many a ruddy throat:
"For the Tree of Laughing Bells
Grew from a bleeding seed
Planted mid enchantment
Played on a harp and reed:
Darkness was the harp--
Chaos-wind the reed;
The fruit of the tree is a bell, blood-red--
The seed was the heart of a fairy, dead.
Part of the bells of the Laughing Tree
Fell to-day at a blast from the reed.
Bring a fallen bell to me.
Go!" the maiden said.
"For the bell will quench our memory,
Our hope,
Our borrowed sorrow;
We will have no thirst for yesterday,
No thought for to-morrow."

The Journey Starts Swiftly

A thousand times ten thousand times
More swift than the sun's swift light
Were the Morning Wings in their flight
On-- On--
West of the Universe,
Thro' the West
To Chaos-night.

He Nears the Goal

How the red bells rang
As I neared the Chaos-shore!
As I flew across to the end of the West
The young bells rang and rang
Above the Chaos roar,
And the Wings of the Morning
Beat in tune
And bore me like a bird along--
And the nearing star turned to a moon--
Gray moon, with a brow of red--
Gray moon with a golden song.
Like a diver after pearls
I plunged to that stifling floor.
It was wide as a giant's wheat-field
An icy, wind-washed shore.
O laughing, proud, but trembling star!
O wind that wounded sore!

He Climbs the Hill Where the Tree Grows

On--
Thro' the gleaming gray
I ran to the storm and clang--
To the red, red hill where the great tree swayed--
And scattered bells like autumn leaves.
How the red bells rang!
My breath within my breast
Was held like a diver's breath--
The leaves were tangled locks of gray--
The boughs of the tree were white and gray,
Shaped like scythes of Death.
The boughs of the tree would sweep and sway--
Sway like scythes of Death.
But it was beautiful!
I knew that all was well.
A thousand bells from a thousand boughs
Each moment bloomed and fell.
On the hill of the wind-swept tree
There were no bells asleep;
They sang beneath my trailing wings
Like rivers sweet and steep.
Deep rock-clefts before my feet
Mighty chimes did keep
And little choirs did keep.

He Receives the Bells

Honeyed, small and fair,
Like flowers, in flowery lands--

Like little maidens' hands--
Two bells fell in my hair,
Two bells caressed my hair.
I pressed them to my purple lips
In the strangling Chaos-air.

He Starts on the Return Journey

On desperate wings and strong,
Two bells within my breast,
I breathed again, I breathed again--
West of the Universe--
West of the skies of the West.
Into the black toward home,
And never a star in sight,
By Faith that is blind I took my way
With my two bosomed blossoms gay
Till a speck in the East was the Milky way:
Till starlit was the night.
And the bells had quenched all memory--
All hope--
All borrowed sorrow:
I had no thirst for yesterday,
No thought for to-morrow.
Like hearts within my breast
The bells would throb to me
And drown the siren stars
That sang enticingly;
My heart became a bell--
Three bells were in my breast,
Three hearts to comfort me.
We reached the daytime happily--

We reached the earth with glee.
In an hour, in an hour it was done!
The wings in their morning flight
Were a thousand times ten thousand times
More swift than beams of light.

He Gives What He Won to the Indian Girl

I panted in the grassy wood;
I kissed the Indian Maid
As she took my wings from me:
With all the grace I could
I gave two throbbing bells to her
From the foot of the Laughing Tree.
And one she pressed to her golden breast
And one, gave back to me.

From Lilies of the valley--
See them fade.
From poppy-blooms all frayed,
From dandelions gray with care,
From pansy-faces, worn and torn,
From morning-glories--
See them fade--
From all things fragile, faint and fair
Are the Wings of the Morning made!

Sweethearts of the Year

Sweetheart Spring

Our Sweetheart, Spring, came softly,
Her gliding hands were fire,
Her lilac breath upon our cheeks
Consumed us with desire.

By her our God began to build,
Began to sow and till.
He laid foundations in our loves
For every good and ill.
We asked Him not for blessing,
We asked Him not for pain--
Still, to the just and unjust
He sent His fire and rain.

Sweetheart Summer

We prayed not, yet she came to us,
The silken, shining one,
On Jacob's noble ladder
Descended from the sun.
She reached our town of Every Day,
Our dry and dusty sod--
We prayed not, yet she brought to us
The misty wine of God.

Sweetheart Autumn

The woods were black and crimson,
The frost-bit flowers were dead,
But Sweetheart Indian Summer came
With love-winds round her head.
While fruits God-given and splendid
Belonged to her domain:
Baskets of corn in perfect ear
And grapes with purple stain,
The treacherous winds persuaded her
Spring Love was in the wood
Altho' the end of love was hers--
Fruition, Motherhood.

Sweetheart Winter

We had done naught of service
To win our Maker's praise.
Yet Sweetheart Winter came to us
To gild our waning days.
Down Jacob's winding ladder
She came from Sunshine Town,
Bearing the sparkling mornings
And clouds of silver-brown;
Bearing the seeds of Springtime.
Upon her snowy seas
Bearing the fairy star-flowers
For baby Christmas trees.

The Sorceress!

I asked her, "Is Aladdin's lamp
Hidden anywhere?"
"Look into your heart," she said,
"Aladdin's lamp is there."

She took my heart with glowing hands.
It burned to dust and air
And smoke and rolling thistledown
Blowing everywhere.

"Follow the thistledown," she said,
"Till doomsday, if you dare,
Over the hills and far away.
Aladdin's lamp is there."

Caught in a Net

Upon her breast her hands and hair
 Were tangled all together.
The moon of June forbade me not--
 The golden night time weather
In balmy sighs commanded me
 To kiss them like a feather.

Her looming hair, her burning hands,
 Were tangled black and white.

My face I buried there. I pray--
 So far from her to-night--
For grace, to dream I kiss her soul
 Amid the black and white.

Eden in Winter

[Supposed to be chanted to some rude instrument at a modern fireplace]

Chant we the story now
Tho' in a house we sleep;
Tho' by a hearth of coals
Vigil to-night we keep.
Chant we the story now,
Of the vague love we knew
When I from out the sea
Rose to the feet of you.

Bird from the cliffs you came,
Flew thro' the snow to me,
Facing the icy blast
There by the icy sea.
How did I reach your feet?
Why should I--at the end
Hold out half-frozen hands
Dumbly to you my friend?
Ne'er had I woman seen,
Ne'er had I seen a flame.
There you piled fagots on,
Heat rose--the blast to tame.
There by the cave-door dark,

Comforting me you cried--
Wailed o'er my wounded knee,
Wept for my rock-torn side.

Up from the South I trailed--
Left regions fierce and fair!
Left all the jungle-trees,
Left the red tiger's lair.
Dream led, I scarce knew why,
Into your North I trod--
Ne'er had I known the snow,
Or the frost-blasted sod.

O how the flakes came down!
O how the fire burned high!
Strange thing to see he was,
Thro' his dry twigs would fly,
Creep there awhile and sleep--
Then wake and bark for fight--
Biting if I too near
Came to his eye so bright.
Then with a will you fed
Wood to his hungry tongue.

Then he did leap and sing--
Dancing the clouds among,
Turning the night to noon,
Stinging my eyes with light,
Making the snow retreat,
Making the cave-house bright.

There were dry fagots piled,
Nuts and dry leaves and roots,

Stores there of furs and hides,
Sweet-barks and grains and fruits.
There wrapped in fur we lay,
Half-burned, half-frozen still--
Ne'er will my soul forget
All the night's bitter chill.
We had not learned to speak,
I was to you a strange
Wolfling or wounded fawn,
Lost from his forest-range.

Thirsting for bloody meat,
Out at the dawn we went.
Weighed with our prey at eve,
Home-came we all forespent.
Comrades and hunters tried
Ere we were maid and man--
Not till the spring awoke
Laughter and speech began.

Whining like forest dogs,
Rustling like budding trees,
Bubbling like thawing springs,
Humming like little bees,
Crooning like Maytime tides,
Chattering parrot words,
Crying the panther's cry,
Chirping like mating birds--
Thus, thus, we learned to speak,
Who mid the snows were dumb,
Nor did we learn to kiss
Until the Spring had come.

Genesis

I was but a half-grown boy,
You were a girl-child slight.
Ah, how weary you were!
You had led in the bullock-fight . . .
We slew the bullock at length
With knives and maces of stone.
And so your feet were torn,
Your lean arms bruised to the bone.

Perhaps 'twas the slain beast's blood
We drank, or a root we ate,
Or our reveling evening bath
In the fall by the garden gate,
But you turned to a witching thing,
Side-glancing, and frightened me;
You purred like a panther's cub,
You sighed like a shell from the sea.

We knelt. I caressed your hair
By the light of the leaping fire:
Your fierce eyes blinked with smoke,
Pine-fumes, that enhanced desire.
I helped to unbraid your hair
In wonder and fear profound:
You were humming your hunting tune
As it swept to the grassy ground.

Our comrades, the shaggy bear,
The tiger with velvet feet,

The lion, crept to the light
Whining for bullock meat.
We fed them and stroked their necks . . .
They took their way to the fen
Where they hunted or hid all night;
No enemies, they, of men.

Evil had entered not
The cobra, since defiled.
He watched, when the beasts had gone
Our kissing and singing wild.
Beautiful friend he was,
Sage, not a tempter grim.
Many a year should pass
Ere Satan should enter him.

He danced while the evening dove
And the nightingale kept in tune.
I sang of the angel sun:
You sang of the angel-moon:
We sang of the ANGEL-CHIEF
Who blew thro' the trees strange breath,
Who helped in the hunt all day
And granted the bullock's death.

O Eve with the fire-lit breast
And child-face red and white!
I heaped the great logs high!
That was our bridal night.

Queen Mab in the Village

Once I loved a fairy,
Queen Mab it was. Her voice
Was like a little Fountain
That bids the birds rejoice.
Her face was wise and solemn,
Her hair was brown and fine.
Her dress was pansy velvet,
A butterfly design.

To see her hover round me
Or walk the hills of air,
Awakened love's deep pulses
And boyhood's first despair;
A passion like a sword-blade
That pierced me thro' and thro':
Her fingers healed the sorrow
Her whisper would renew.
We sighed and reigned and feasted
Within a hollow tree,
We vowed our love was boundless,
Eternal as the sea.

She banished from her kingdom
The mortal boy I grew--
So tall and crude and noisy,
I killed grasshoppers too.
I threw big rocks at pigeons,
I plucked and tore apart
The weeping, wailing daisies,

And broke my lady's heart.
At length I grew to manhood,
I scarcely could believe
I ever loved the lady,
Or caused her court to grieve,
Until a dream came to me,
One bleak first night of Spring,
Ere tides of apple blossoms
Rolled in o'er everything,
While rain and sleet and snowbanks
Were still a-vexing men,
Ere robin and his comrades
Were nesting once again.

I saw Mab's Book of Judgment--
Its clasps were iron and stone,
Its leaves were mammoth ivory,
Its boards were mammoth bone,--
Hid in her seaside mountains,
Forgotten or unkept,
Beneath its mighty covers
Her wrath against me slept.
And deeply I repented
Of brash and boyish crime,
Of murder of things lovely
Now and in olden time.
I cursed my vain ambition,
My would-be worldly days,
And craved the paths of wonder,
Of dewy dawns and fays.
I cried, "Our love was boundless,
Eternal as the sea,
O Queen, reverse the sentence,

Come back and master me!"

The book was by the cliff-side
Upon its edge upright.
I laid me by it softly,
And wept throughout the night.
And there at dawn I saw it,
No book now, but a door,
Upon its panels written,
"Judgment is no more."
The bolt flew back with thunder,
I saw within that place
A mermaid wrapped in seaweed
With Mab's immortal face,
Yet grown now to a woman,
A woman to the knee.
She cried, she clasped me fondly,
We soon were in the sea.

Ah, she was wise and subtle,
And gay and strong and sleek,
We chained the wicked sword-fish,
We played at hide and seek.
We floated on the water,
We heard the dawn-wind sing,
I made from ocean-wonders,
Her bridal wreath and ring.
All mortal girls were shadows,
All earth-life but a mist,
When deep beneath the maelstrom,
The mermaid's heart I kissed.

I woke beside the church-door
Of our small inland town,
Bowing to a maiden
In a pansy-velvet gown,
Who had not heard of fairies,
Yet seemed of love to dream.
We planned an earthly cottage
Beside an earthly stream.
Our wedding long is over,
With toil the years fill up,
Yet in the evening silence,
We drink a deep-sea cup.
Nothing the fay remembers,
Yet when she turns to me,
We meet beneath the whirlpool,
We swim the golden sea.

The Dandelion

O dandelion, rich and haughty,
King of village flowers!
Each day is coronation time,
You have no humble hours.
I like to see you bring a troop
To beat the blue-grass spears,
To scorn the lawn-mower that would be
Like fate's triumphant shears.
Your yellow heads are cut away,
It seems your reign is o'er.
By noon you raise a sea of stars
More golden than before.

The Light o' the Moon

[How different people and different animals look upon the moon: showing that each creature finds in it his own mood and disposition]

The Old Horse in the City

The moon's a peck of corn. It lies
Heaped up for me to eat.
I wish that I might climb the path
And taste that supper sweet.

Men feed me straw and scanty grain
And beat me till I'm sore.
Some day I'll break the halter-rope
And smash the stable-door,

Run down the street and mount the hill
Just as the corn appears.
I've seen it rise at certain times
For years and years and years.

What the Hyena Said

The moon is but a golden skull,
She mounts the heavens now,
And Moon-Worms, mighty Moon-Worms
Are wreathed around her brow.

The Moon-Worms are a doughty race:
They eat her gray and golden face.
Her eye-sockets dead, and molding head:
These caverns are their dwelling-place.

The Moon-Worms, serpents of the skies,
From the great hollows of her eyes
Behold all souls, and they are wise:
With tiny, keen and icy eyes,
Behold how each man sins and dies.

When Earth in gold-corruption lies
Long dead, the moon-worm butterflies
On cyclone wings will reach this place--
Yea, rear their brood on earth's dead face.

What the Snow Man Said

The Moon's a snowball. See the drifts
Of white that cross the sphere.
The Moon's a snowball, melted down
A dozen times a year.

Yet rolled again in hot July
When all my days are done
And cool to greet the weary eye
After the scorching sun.

The moon's a piece of winter fair
Renewed the year around,
Behold it, deathless and unstained,
Above the grimy ground!

It rolls on high so brave and white
Where the clear air-rivers flow,
Proclaiming Christmas all the time
And the glory of the snow!

What the Scare-crow Said

The dim-winged spirits of the night
Do fear and serve me well.
They creep from out the hedges of
The garden where I dwell.

I wave my arms across the walk.
The troops obey the sign,
And bring me shimmering shadow-robes
And cups of cowslip-wine.

Then dig a treasure called the moon,
A very precious thing,
And keep it in the air for me
Because I am a King.

What Grandpa Mouse Said

The moon's a holy owl-queen.
She keeps them in a jar
Under her arm till evening,
Then sallies forth to war.

She pours the owls upon us.
They hoot with horrid noise
And eat the naughty mousie-girls
And wicked mousie-boys.

So climb the moonvine every night
And to the owl-queen pray:
Leave good green cheese by moonlit trees
For her to take away.

And never squeak, my children,
Nor gnaw the smoke-house door:
The owl-queen then will love us
And send her birds no more.

The Beggar Speaks

"What Mister Moon Said to Me."

Come, eat the bread of idleness,
Come, sit beside the spring:
Some of the flowers will keep awake,
Some of the birds will sing.

Come, eat the bread no man has sought
For half a hundred years:
Men hurry so they have no griefs,
Nor even idle tears:

They hurry so they have no loves:
They cannot curse nor laugh--
Their hearts die in their youth with neither
Grave nor epitaph.

My bread would make them careless,
And never quite on time--
Their eyelids would be heavy,
Their fancies full of rhyme:

Each soul a mystic rose-tree,
Or a curious incense tree:

    .   .   .   .

Come, eat the bread of idleness,
Said Mister Moon to me.

What the Forester Said

The moon is but a candle-glow
That flickers thro' the gloom:
The starry space, a castle hall:
And Earth, the children's room,
Where all night long the old trees stand
To watch the streams asleep:
Grandmothers guarding trundle-beds:
Good shepherds guarding sheep.

A Net to Snare the Moonlight

[What the Man of Faith said]

The dew, the rain and moonlight
All prove our Father's mind.
The dew, the rain and moonlight
Descend to bless mankind.

Come, let us see that all men
Have land to catch the rain,
Have grass to snare the spheres of dew,
And fields spread for the grain.

Yea, we would give to each poor man
Ripe wheat and poppies red,--
A peaceful place at evening
With the stars just overhead:

A net to snare the moonlight,
A sod spread to the sun,
A place of toil by daytime,
Of dreams when toil is done.

Beyond the Moon

[Written to the Most Beautiful Woman in the World]

My Sweetheart is the TRUTH BEYOND THE MOON,
And never have I been in love with Woman,
Always aspiring to be set in tune
With one who is invisible, inhuman.

O laughing girl, cold TRUTH has stepped between,
Spoiling the fevers of your virgin face:
Making your shining eyes but lead and clay,
Mocking your brilliant brain and lady's grace.

TRUTH haunted me the day I wooed and lost,
The day I wooed and won, or wooed in play:
Tho' you were Juliet or Rosalind,
Thus shall it be, forever and a day.

I doubt my vows, tho' sworn on my own blood,
Tho' I draw toward you weeping, soul to soul,
I have a lonely goal beyond the moon;
Ay, beyond Heaven and Hell, I have a goal!

The Song of the Garden-Toad

Down, down beneath the daisy beds,
O hear the cries of pain!
And moaning on the cinder-path
They're blind amid the rain.
Can murmurs of the worms arise
To higher hearts than mine?
I wonder if that gardener hears
Who made the mold all fine
And packed each gentle seedling down
So carefully in line?
I watched the red rose reaching up
To ask him if he heard
Those cries that stung the evening earth
Till all the rose-roots stirred.
She asked him if he felt the hate
That burned beneath them there.
She asked him if he heard the curse
Of worms in black despair.
He kissed the rose. What did it mean?
What of the rose's prayer?
Down, down where rain has never come
They fight in burning graves,
Bleeding and drinking blood
Within those venom-caves.
Blaspheming still the gardener's name,
They live and hate and go.
I wonder if the gardener heard
The rose that told him so?

A Gospel of Beauty:--

I recited these three poems more than any others
in my late mendicant preaching tour through the West.
Taken as a triad, they hold in solution my theory
of American civilization.

The Proud Farmer

[In memory of E. S. Frazee, Rush County, Indiana]

Into the acres of the newborn state
He poured his strength, and plowed his ancient name,
And, when the traders followed him, he stood
Towering above their furtive souls and tame.

That brow without a stain, that fearless eye
Oft left the passing stranger wondering
To find such knighthood in the sprawling land,
To see a democrat well-nigh a king.

He lived with liberal hand, with guests from far,
With talk and joke and fellowship to spare,--
Watching the wide world's life from sun to sun,

Lining his walls with books from everywhere.
He read by night, he built his world by day.
The farm and house of God to him were one.
For forty years he preached and plowed and wrought--
A statesman in the fields, who bent to none.

His plowmen-neighbors were as lords to him.
His was an ironside, democratic pride.
He served a rigid Christ, but served him well--
And, for a lifetime, saved the countryside.

Here lie the dead, who gave the church their best
Under his fiery preaching of the word.
They sleep with him beneath the ragged grass . . .
The village withers, by his voice unstirred.

And tho' his tribe be scattered to the wind
From the Atlantic to the China sea,
Yet do they think of that bright lamp he burned
Of family worth and proud integrity.

And many a sturdy grandchild hears his name
In reverence spoken, till he feels akin
To all the lion-eyed who built the world--
And lion-dreams begin to burn within.

The Illinois Village

O you who lose the art of hope,
Whose temples seem to shrine a lie,
Whose sidewalks are but stones of fear,
Who weep that Liberty must die,
Turn to the little prairie towns,
Your higher hope shall yet begin.
On every side awaits you there
Some gate where glory enters in.

Yet when I see the flocks of girls,
Watching the Sunday train go thro'
(As tho' the whole wide world went by)
With eyes that long to travel too,
I sigh, despite my soul made glad
By cloudy dresses and brown hair,
Sigh for the sweet life wrenched and torn
By thundering commerce, fierce and bare.
Nymphs of the wheat these girls should be:
Kings of the grove, their lovers strong.
Why are they not inspired, aflame?
This beauty calls for valiant song--
For men to carve these fairy-forms
And faces in a fountain-frieze;
Dancers that own immortal hours;
Painters that work upon their knees;
Maids, lovers, friends, so deep in life,
So deep in love and poet's deeds,
The railroad is a thing disowned,
The city but a field of weeds.

Who can pass a village church
By night in these clean prairie lands
Without a touch of Spirit-power?
So white and fixed and cool it stands--
A thing from some strange fairy-town,
A pious amaranthine flower,
Unsullied by the winds, as pure
As jade or marble, wrought this hour:--
Rural in form, foursquare and plain,
And yet our sister, the new moon,
Makes it a praying wizard's dream.
The trees that watch at dusty noon
Breaking its sharpest lines, veil not
The whiteness it reflects from God,
Flashing like Spring on many an eye,
Making clean flesh, that once was clod.

Who can pass a district school
Without the hope that there may wait
Some baby-heart the books shall flame
With zeal to make his playmates great,
To make the whole wide village gleam
A strangely carved celestial gem,
Eternal in its beauty-light,
The Artist's town of Bethlehem!

On the Building of Springfield

Let not our town be large, remembering
That little Athens was the Muses' home,
That Oxford rules the heart of London still,
That Florence gave the Renaissance to Rome.

Record it for the grandson of your son--
A city is not builded in a day:
Our little town cannot complete her soul
Till countless generations pass away.

Now let each child be joined as to a church
To her perpetual hopes, each man ordained:
Let every street be made a reverent aisle
Where Music grows and Beauty is unchained.

Let Science and Machinery and Trade
Be slaves of her, and make her all in all,
Building against our blatant, restless time
An unseen, skilful, medieval wall.

Let every citizen be rich toward God.
Let Christ the beggar, teach divinity.
Let no man rule who holds his money dear.
Let this, our city, be our luxury.

We should build parks that students from afar
Would choose to starve in, rather than go home,
Fair little squares, with Phidian ornament,
Food for the spirit, milk and honeycomb.

Songs shall be sung by us in that good day,
Songs we have written, blood within the rhyme
Beating, as when Old England still was glad,--
The purple, rich Elizabethan time.

   .   .   .   .   .

Say, is my prophecy too fair and far?
I only know, unless her faith be high,
The soul of this, our Nineveh, is doomed,
Our little Babylon will surely die.

Some city on the breast of Illinois
No wiser and no better at the start
By faith shall rise redeemed, by faith shall rise
Bearing the western glory in her heart.

The genius of the Maple, Elm and Oak,
The secret hidden in each grain of corn,
The glory that the prairie angels sing
At night when sons of Life and Love are born,

Born but to struggle, squalid and alone,
Broken and wandering in their early years.
When will they make our dusty streets their goal,
Within our attics hide their sacred tears?

When will they start our vulgar blood athrill
With living language, words that set us free?
When will they make a path of beauty clear
Between our riches and our liberty?

We must have many Lincoln-hearted men.

A city is not builded in a day.
And they must do their work, and come and go
While countless generations pass away.

Nicholas Vachel Lindsay (1879-1931):
(Vachel is pronounced Vay-chul, that is, it rhymes with 'Rachel').

Vachel Lindsay, of Springfield, Illinois, is best known for his efforts
to restore the vocal tradition to poetry. He made a journey on foot
as far as New Mexico, taking along copies of a pamphlet,
"Rhymes to be Traded for Bread", for the purpose the title suggests.
He wrote of this journey in "Adventures while Preaching the Gospel of
Beauty".

"The Eagle that is Forgotten" and "The Congo" are his best-known poems,
and appear in his first two volumes of verse, "General William Booth
Enters into Heaven" (1913) and "The Congo" (1914).

As a sidenote, he became close friends with the poet Sara Teasdale
(well worth reading in her own right--perhaps the better poet),
and his third volume of verse, "The Chinese Nightingale" (1917),
is dedicated to her. In turn, she wrote a memorial verse for him
after he committed suicide in 1931.

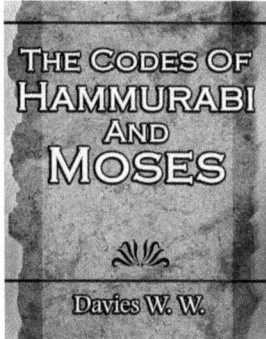

The Codes Of Hammurabi And Moses
W. W. Davies

QTY

The discovery of the Hammurabi Code is one of the greatest achievements of archaeology, and is of paramount interest, not only to the student of the Bible, but also to all those interested in ancient history...

Religion   ISBN: *1-59462-338-4*   Pages:132
MSRP $12.95

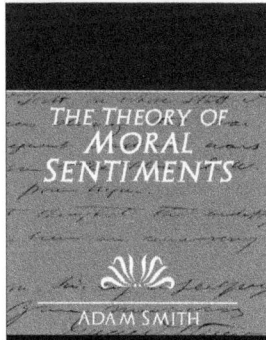

The Theory of Moral Sentiments
Adam Smith

QTY

This work from 1749. contains original theories of conscience amd moral judgment and it is the foundation for systemof morals.

Philosophy ISBN: *1-59462-777-0*   Pages:536
MSRP $19.95

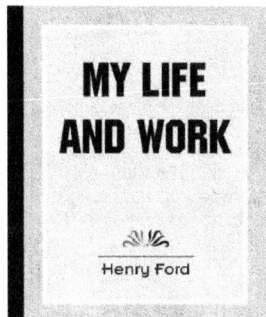

Jessica's First Prayer
Hesba Stretton

QTY

In a screened and secluded corner of one of the many railway-bridges which span the streets of London there could be seen a few years ago, from five o'clock every morning until half past eight, a tidily set-out coffee-stall, consisting of a trestle and board, upon which stood two large tin cans, with a small fire of charcoal burning under each so as to keep the coffee boiling during the early hours of the morning when the work-people were thronging into the city on their way to their daily toil...

Pages:84

Childrens   ISBN: *1-59462-373-2*   *MSRP $9.95*

My Life and Work
Henry Ford

QTY

Henry Ford revolutionized the world with his implementation of mass production for the Model T automobile. Gain valuable business insight into his life and work with his own auto-biography... "We have only started on our development of our country we have not as yet, with all our talk of wonderful progress, done more than scratch the surface. The progress has been wonderful enough but..."

Pages:300

Biographies/   ISBN: *1-59462-198-5*   *MSRP $21.95*

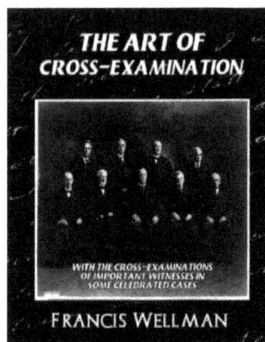

The Art of Cross-Examination
Francis Wellman

QTY

I presume it is the experience of every author, after his first book is published upon an important subject, to be almost overwhelmed with a wealth of ideas and illustrations which could readily have been included in his book, and which to his own mind, at least, seem to make a second edition inevitable. Such certainly was the case with me; and when the first edition had reached its sixth impression in five months, I rejoiced to learn that it seemed to my publishers that the book had met with a sufficiently favorable reception to justify a second and considerably enlarged edition. ...

Pages:412

Reference   **ISBN: *1-59462-647-2***   *MSRP $19.95*

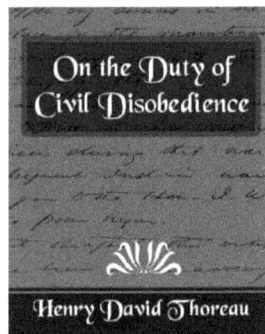

On the Duty of Civil Disobedience
Henry David Thoreau

QTY

Thoreau wrote his famous essay, On the Duty of Civil Disobedience, as a protest against an unjust but popular war and the immoral but popular institution of slave-owning. He did more than write—he declined to pay his taxes, and was hauled off to gaol in consequence. Who can say how much this refusal of his hastened the end of the war and of slavery ?

Law   **ISBN: *1-59462-747-9***   **Pages:48**

MSRP $7.45

Dream Psychology Psychoanalysis for Beginners
Sigmund Freud

QTY

Sigmund Freud, born Sigismund Schlomo Freud (May 6, 1856 - September 23, 1939), was a Jewish-Austrian neurologist and psychiatrist who co-founded the psychoanalytic school of psychology. Freud is best known for his theories of the unconscious mind, especially involving the mechanism of repression; his redefinition of sexual desire as mobile and directed towards a wide variety of objects; and his therapeutic techniques, especially his understanding of transference in the therapeutic relationship and the presumed value of dreams as sources of insight into unconscious desires.

Pages:196

Psychology   **ISBN: *1-59462-905-6***   *MSRP $15.45*

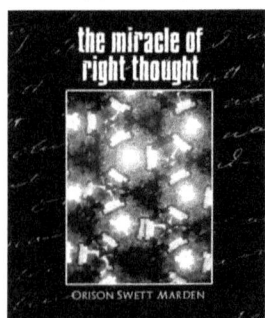

The Miracle of Right Thought
Orison Swett Marden

QTY

Believe with all of your heart that you will do what you were made to do. When the mind has once formed the habit of holding cheerful, happy, prosperous pictures, it will not be easy to form the opposite habit. It does not matter how improbable or how far away this realization may see, or how dark the prospects may be, if we visualize them as best we can, as vividly as possible, hold tenaciously to them and vigorously struggle to attain them, they will gradually become actualized, realized in the life. But a desire, a longing without endeavor, a yearning abandoned or held indifferently will vanish without realization.

Pages:360

Self Help   **ISBN: *1-59462-644-8***   *MSRP $25.45*

www.bookjungle.com *email: sales@bookjungle.com fax: 630-214-0564 mail: Book Jungle PO Box 2226 Champaign, IL 61825*

QTY

☐	**The Rosicrucian Cosmo-Conception Mystic Christianity** *by Max Heindel* ISBN: *1-59462-188-8* **$38.95** *The Rosicrucian Cosmo-conception is not dogmatic, neither does it appeal to any other authority than the reason of the student. It is: not controversial, but is: sent forth in the, hope that it may help to clear..* New Age/Religion Pages 646
☐	**Abandonment To Divine Providence** *by Jean-Pierre de Caussade* ISBN: *1-59462-228-0* **$25.95** *"The Rev. Jean Pierre de Caussade was one of the most remarkable spiritual writers of the Society of Jesus in France in the 18th Century. His death took place at Toulouse in 1751. His works have gone through many editions and have been republished...* Inspirational/Religion Pages 400
☐	**Mental Chemistry** *by Charles Haanel* ISBN: *1-59462-192-6* **$23.95** *Mental Chemistry allows the change of material conditions by combining and appropriately utilizing the power of the mind. Much like applied chemistry creates something new and unique out of careful combinations of chemicals the mastery of mental chemistry...* New Age Pages 354
☐	**The Letters of Robert Browning and Elizabeth Barret Barrett 1845-1846 vol II** ISBN: *1-59462-193-4* **$35.95** *by Robert Browning and Elizabeth Barrett* Biographies Pages 596
☐	**Gleanings In Genesis (volume I)** *by Arthur W. Pink* ISBN: *1-59462-130-6* **$27.45** *Appropriately has Genesis been termed "the seed plot of the Bible" for in it we have, in germ form, almost all of the great doctrines which are afterwards fully developed in the books of Scripture which follow...* Religion/Inspirational Pages 420
☐	**The Master Key** *by L. W. de Laurence* ISBN: *1-59462-001-6* **$30.95** *In no branch of human knowledge has there been a more lively increase of the spirit of research during the past few years than in the study of Psychology, Concentration and Mental Discipline. The requests for authentic lessons in Thought Control, Mental Discipline and...* New Age/Business Pages 422
☐	**The Lesser Key Of Solomon Goetia** *by L. W. de Laurence* ISBN: *1-59462-092-X* **$9.95** *This translation of the first book of the "Lemegton" which is now for the first time made accessible to students of Talismanic Magic was done, after careful collation and edition, from numerous Ancient Manuscripts in Hebrew, Latin, and French...* New Age/Occult Pages 92
☐	**Rubaiyat Of Omar Khayyam** *by Edward Fitzgerald* ISBN:*1-59462-332-5* **$13.95** *Edward Fitzgerald, whom the world has already learned, in spite of his own efforts to remain within the shadow of anonymity, to look upon as one of the rarest poets of the century, was born at Bredfield, in Suffolk, on the 31st of March, 1809. He was the third son of John Purcell...* Music Pages 172
☐	**Ancient Law** *by Henry Maine* ISBN: *1-59462-128-4* **$29.95** *The chief object of the following pages is to indicate some of the earliest ideas of mankind, as they are reflected in Ancient Law, and to point out the relation of those ideas to modern thought.* Religion/History Pages 452
☐	**Far-Away Stories** *by William J. Locke* ISBN: *1-59462-129-2* **$19.45** *"Good wine needs no bush," but a collection of mixed vintages does. And this book is just such a collection. Some of the stories I do not want to remain buried for ever in the museum files of dead magazine-numbers an author's not unpardonable vanity..."* Fiction Pages 272
☐	**Life of David Crockett** *by David Crockett* ISBN: *1-59462-250-7* **$27.45** *"Colonel David Crockett was one of the most remarkable men of the times in which he lived. Born in humble life, but gifted with a strong will, an indomitable courage, and unremitting perseverance...* Biographies/New Age Pages 424
☐	**Lip-Reading** *by Edward Nitchie* ISBN: *1-59462-206-X* **$25.95** *Edward B. Nitchie, founder of the New York School for the Hard of Hearing, now the Nitchie School of Lip-Reading, Inc, wrote "LIP-READING Principles and Practice". The development and perfecting of this meritorious work on lip-reading was an undertaking...* How-to Pages 400
☐	**A Handbook of Suggestive Therapeutics, Applied Hypnotism, Psychic Science** ISBN: *1-59462-214-0* **$24.95** *by Henry Munro* Health/New Age/Health/Self-help Pages 376
☐	**A Doll's House: and Two Other Plays** *by Henrik Ibsen* ISBN: *1-59462-112-8* **$19.95** *Henrik Ibsen created this classic when in revolutionary 1848 Rome. Introducing some striking concepts in playwriting for the realist genre, this play has been studied the world over.* Fiction/Classics/Plays 308
☐	**The Light of Asia** *by sir Edwin Arnold* ISBN: *1-59462-204-3* **$13.95** *In this poetic masterpiece, Edwin Arnold describes the life and teachings of Buddha. The man who was to become known as Buddha to the world was born as Prince Gautama of India but he rejected the worldly riches and abandoned the reigns of power when...* Religion/History/Biographies Pages 170
☐	**The Complete Works of Guy de Maupassant** *by Guy de Maupassant* ISBN: *1-59462-157-8* **$16.95** *"For days and days, nights and nights, I had dreamed of that first kiss which was to consecrate our engagement, and I knew not on what spot I should put my lips..."* Fiction/Classics Pages 240
☐	**The Art of Cross-Examination** *by Francis L. Wellman* ISBN: *1-59462-309-0* **$26.95** *Written by a renowned trial lawyer, Wellman imparts his experience and uses case studies to explain how to use psychology to extract desired information through questioning.* How-to/Science/Reference Pages 408
☐	**Answered or Unanswered?** *by Louisa Vaughan* ISBN: *1-59462-248-5* **$10.95** *Miracles of Faith in China* Religion Pages 112
☐	**The Edinburgh Lectures on Mental Science (1909)** *by Thomas* ISBN: *1-59462-008-3* **$11.95** *This book contains the substance of a course of lectures recently given by the writer in the Queen Street Hail, Edinburgh. Its purpose is to indicate the Natural Principles governing the relation between Mental Action and Material Conditions...* New Age/Psychology Pages 148
☐	**Ayesha** *by H. Rider Haggard* ISBN: *1-59462-301-5* **$24.95** *Verily and indeed it is the unexpected that happens! Probably if there was one person upon the earth from whom the Editor of this, and of a certain previous history, did not expect to hear again...* Classics Pages 380
☐	**Ayala's Angel** *by Anthony Trollope* ISBN: *1-59462-352-X* **$29.95** *The two girls were both pretty, but Lucy who was twenty-one who supposed to be simple and comparatively unattractive, whereas Ayala was credited, as her Bombwhat romantic name might show, with poetic charm and a taste for romance. Ayala when her father died was nineteen...* Fiction Pages 484
☐	**The American Commonwealth** *by James Bryce* ISBN: *1-59462-286-8* **$34.45** *An interpretation of American democratic political theory. It examines political mechanics and society from the perspective of Scotsman James Bryce* Politics Pages 572
☐	**Stories of the Pilgrims** *by Margaret P. Pumphrey* ISBN: *1-59462-116-0* **$17.95** *This book explores pilgrims religious oppression in England as well as their escape to Holland and eventual crossing to America on the Mayflower, and their early days in New England...* History Pages 268

www.bookjungle.com *email: sales@bookjungle.com fax: 630-214-0564 mail: Book Jungle PO Box 2226 Champaign, IL 61825*

QTY

The Fasting Cure *by Sinclair Upton* **ISBN: 1-59462-222-1** **$13.95**
In the Cosmopolitan Magazine for May, 1910, and in the Contemporary Review (London) for April, 1910, I published an article dealing with my experiences in fasting. I have written a great many magazine articles, but never one which attracted so much attention... New Age/Self Help/Health Pages 164

Hebrew Astrology *by Sepharial* **ISBN: 1-59462-308-2** **$13.45**
In these days of advanced thinking it is a matter of common observation that we have left many of the old landmarks behind and that we are now pressing forward to greater heights and to a wider horizon than that which represented the mind-content of our progenitors... Astrology Pages 144

Thought Vibration or The Law of Attraction in the Thought World **ISBN: 1-59462-127-6** **$12.95**
by William Walker Atkinson *Psychology/Religion Pages 144*

Optimism *by Helen Keller* **ISBN: 1-59462-108-X** **$15.95**
Helen Keller was blind, deaf, and mute since 19 months old, yet famously learned how to overcome these handicaps, communicate with the world, and spread her lectures promoting optimism. An inspiring read for everyone... Biographies/Inspirational Pages 84

Sara Crewe *by Frances Burnett* **ISBN: 1-59462-360-0** **$9.45**
In the first place, Miss Minchin lived in London. Her home was a large, dull, tall one, in a large, dull square, where all the houses were alike, and all the sparrows were alike, and where all the door-knockers made the same heavy sound... Childrens/Classic Pages 88

The Autobiography of Benjamin Franklin *by Benjamin Franklin* **ISBN: 1-59462-135-7** **$24.95**
The Autobiography of Benjamin Franklin has probably been more extensively read than any other American historical work, and no other book of its kind has had such ups and downs of fortune. Franklin lived for many years in England, where he was agent... Biographies/History Pages 332

Name	
Email	
Telephone	
Address	
City, State ZIP	

☐ **Credit Card**   ☐ **Check / Money Order**

Credit Card Number	
Expiration Date	
Signature	

Please Mail to: Book Jungle
PO Box 2226
Champaign, IL 61825
or Fax to: 630-214-0564

ORDERING INFORMATION
web: *www.bookjungle.com*
email: *sales@bookjungle.com*
fax: *630-214-0564*
mail: *Book Jungle PO Box 2226 Champaign, IL 61825*
or PayPal *to sales@bookjungle.com*

Please contact us for bulk discounts

DIRECT-ORDER TERMS

**20% Discount if You Order
Two or More Books**
Free Domestic Shipping!
Accepted: Master Card, Visa,
Discover, American Express

www.ingramcontent.com/pod-product-compliance
Lightning Source LLC
Chambersburg PA
CBHW050356100426
42739CB00015BB/3412